FLAMINGOS

Maddie Gibbs

PowerKiDS
press™
New York

For Yang

Published in 2011 by The Rosen Publishing Group, Inc.
29 East 21st Street, New York, NY 10010

First Edition

Editor: Amelie von Zumbusch
Layout Design: Greg Tucker

Photo Credits: Cover, pp. 5, 13, 15, 17, 19, 24 (top left), 24 (bottom left), 24 (bottom right) Shutterstock.com; p. 6–7 Stockbyte/Thinkstock; p. 9 Anup Shah/Digital Vision/Thinkstock; p. 10–11 Comstock/Thinkstock; pp. 21, 24 (top right) Hemera/Thinkstock; p. 23 Oxford Scientific/Getty Images.

Library of Congress Cataloging-in-Publication Data

Gibbs, Maddie.
 Flamingos / by Maddie Gibbs. — 1st ed.
    p. cm. — (Safari animals)
 Includes bibliographical references and index.
 ISBN 978-1-4488-3184-5 (library binding) — ISBN 978-1-4488-3185-2 (pbk.) —
 ISBN 978-1-4488-3186-9 (6-pack)
 1. Flamingos—Africa—Juvenile literature. I. Title.
 QL696.C56.G53 2011
 598.3'5—dc22
                                        2010024467

Manufactured in the United States of America

CPSIA Compliance Information: Batch #WW11PK: For Further Information contact Rosen Publishing, New York, New York at 1-800-237-9932

Contents

These big birds are flamingos.
Flamingos are waterbirds.

Lesser flamingos, such as these, can be found in Africa's lakes.

Greater flamingos live in Africa, too. They are the biggest kind of flamingo.

A flamingo can measure up to 65 inches (165 cm) from wing tip to wing tip.

Flamingos have long necks.
They have big **bills**.

13

Flamingos use their bills to suck small animals out of the water.

15

Flamingos live in big **flocks**. A flock can have as many as a million birds!

Flamingos pick **mates** with which to have babies. The females lay eggs.

Flamingo **chicks** break out of these eggs. The chicks are white or gray.

21

Both flamingo mothers and fathers feed and look after their chicks.

Words to Know

bill

chick

flock

mates

Index

Web Sites

Due to the changing nature of Internet links, PowerKids Press has developed an online list of Web sites related to the subject of this book. This site is updated regularly. Please use this link to access the list:
www.powerkidslinks.com/safari/flam/